A HINDU FAMILY IN BRITAIN

MAN AND RELIGION SERIES
Part I/
Families and Faiths

THE
RELIGIOUS EDUCATION PRESS
LTD
a member of the Pergamon Group
Headington Hill Hall
OXFORD

A HINDU FAMILY IN BRITAIN

Peter Bridger

ACKNOWLEDGEMENTS

The author wishes to thank the following for all their help and assistance in planning and writing this book, and for so readily providing the facilities for obtaining information and material.

The High Commission of India, in particular members of the Education and Library Departments.
The Librarian, and his assistants, of the Commonwealth Institute.
The Chief Education Officer, Head Teachers and Staff of Coventry.
Mr. and Mrs. S. N. Bharadwaj.
Mrs. Shah and Mr. Ruprah, of Southall.
The Reverend A. Gilmore.
Miss B. C. Swann.
Miss O. B. Knight.
June, Neil and Hilary, and many Hindu and British friends.

Peter Bridger
is Senior Lecturer in Education
at Eastbourne College of Education

Drawings and Design
Keith Clements

Endpaper drawn from decorative relief panels on mud walls in houses in Gujarat.

MAN AND RELIGION SERIES
General Editor   Ronald Dingwall
Art Director   Keith Clements

THE
RELIGIOUS EDUCATION PRESS
LTD
a member of the Pergamon Group

OXFORD   NEW YORK
TORONTO   SYDNEY   BRAUNSCHWEIG

First published 1969
© 1969 Peter Bridger
Reprinted 1973
Library of Congress Catalog Card No. 72-87269

Made and printed in Great Britain by
A Wheaton and Company   Exeter   Devon

08 006905 3 Limp Cover
08 006312 8 Hard Cover

IN THIS BOOK

1 A LETTER FROM THE PRESIDENT OF THE HINDU CENTRE LONDON

Dear Young Friends of Great Britain,

It is with the greatest pleasure that I am introducing you to Mr. P. Bridger's very interesting book, **"A Hindu Family in Britain."**

I have had the honour of going through the whole of the manuscript of this book and I can say with confidence that Mr. Bridger has been able to produce an excellent book containing very clear descriptions of the Hindu way of life.

Different ways of life keep groups and peoples away from one another. Knowledge can remove or very much weaken false ideas. In my opinion Mr. Bridger has tried to strike at the very root of the problem.

He has collected as much information about the immigrant Hindu community in Great Britain as could be possible for the size of this book.

The author has also tried to keep you informed of the new changes taking place among the Hindu people in Great Britain.

I believe this book is bound to make a valuable contribution towards goodwill and mutual understanding.

Greetings to you all.

S N Bharadwaj

S. N. Bharadwaj
President, Hindu Centre,
London.

2

OUR HINDU FAMILY

India is a secular state of 490 million people, but the Indian people follow a number of religions:

Hinduism, Islam, Buddhism, Christianity, Sikhism, Jainism, Zoroastrianism, and Judaism.

The majority of Indians follow **Hinduism** which does not set out to win others to its faith as do Islam and Christianity.

Here is our Hindu family: four people from a population of 320 million Hindus.

Narinder Shah   **Lalita Shah**

Nina Shah   **Nimish Shah**

They now live in London, but they could have chosen to live in any of the big cities or towns in Britain.

3 THE UNIVERSAL DECLARATION OF HUMAN RIGHTS

Most of the nations of the world have agreed to try to work together for the good of other nations and of themselves.

In 1948 they agreed to the ideas in a document called **"The Universal Declaration of Human Rights."** Some of these are printed below.

1. **All human beings** are born free and equal in dignity and rights.

2. **Everyone** is entitled to all the rights and freedoms set forth in this Declaration, without distinction of any kind, such as race, colour, sex, language, religion, political or other opinion national or social origin, property, birth or other status.

3. **Everyone** has the right to life, liberty and security of person.

4. **All** are equal before the law and are entitled without any discrimination to equal protection of the law.

5. **Everyone** has the right to leave any country including his own and to return to his country.

6. **No one** shall be deprived of his nationality nor denied the right to change his nationality.

7. **Everyone** has the right to freedom of opinion and expression.

8. **Everyone** has the right to work, to free choice of employment, to just and favourable conditions of work, and to protection against unemployment.

9. **Education** shall promote understanding, tolerance and friendship among all nations, racial or religious groups.

10. **Everyone** has the right freely to

participate in the cultural life of the community, to enjoy the arts and to share in scientific advancement and its benefits.

I wonder whether you can remember and understand these and discuss them with your friends and your teacher. Can you discover whether these statements hold true today in our country?

Photo: United Nations.

OF HUMAN RIGHTS

540 miles above India
Astronaut's-eye view from Gemini Space Capsule.

Photo: NASA.

4 BOEING 707

A magic carpet! You don't believe in that. But I wonder what picture of India you would have in your mind if you flew out there, not on a magic carpet but in a Boeing 707.

Would it be a picture of a snake charmer and his weird music? Or of the beautiful Taj Mahal, built of marble by an Emperor as a memorial to his favourite wife? Or again of a man in a turban or of a woman in a colourful sari? Or even of a man lying on a bed of nails?

These pictures may be true of your idea of India, but, of course, they do not tell you anything about the ordinary man or woman, boy or girl who live in India, neither do they help you to understand the Indian family who may be living next door to you, or the Hindu boy or girl who may share your school life with you.

This book sets out in a small way to give as true a picture as possible of the way in which our Hindu neighbours and friends are living in Britain. But it can only give a surface picture of the life of a Hindu family living here. You have to be a Hindu really to understand his way of thinking, but we can all try to know more about him and his family, and to make them feel welcome when the opportunity occurs.

As there are many different kinds of English people, so are there many different kinds of Hindus. Just as we think about the world around us in different ways, so do they. They do things in different ways, so do we. They seek a way of living, so do we.

In this book, we shall see how our Indian family decided to leave their own country and travel hundreds of miles to settle down in a

strange land. We shall also discover some of their traditions and customs which they either continue in Britain or adapt to the British way of life.

The Map of India shows where our Hindu family lived and where hundreds of other Hindus once lived before they settled in Britain. They have travelled about four thousand miles to come here.

Now let's find out something about our immigrant friends by going on an imaginary journey to the village they have left near **Baroda**.

5 AT HOME IN INDIA

As you land from the Boeing 707 at **Bombay** and are then taken by car to a village north of the city in the province of **Gujarat**, you find the home of the **Shah** family. Their village is in a hilly area surrounded on all sides, north, east, south and west, by other villages two to five miles away.

As you look round the village you guess that with **Narinder** and **Lalita** there are just over a thousand other villagers. Many of the families have about six people living in the family house.

You are told by **Nimish** and **Nina** that the chief work of the villagers is cattle-rearing, cultivating the land and stone-cutting.

The village is situated on a plain surrounded by hillocks with a river running south and a National Highway built in the north for fast traffic.

The soil is partly black and rocky and partly grey; it is poor and thin, and is mainly suitable as good pasture-land for cattle.

The weather is cold from October to the end of February and the hot weather begins from March and continues to the end of June. In summer the temperature varies from 12°C(54°F) to 47°C(117°F) and in the winter from 6°C(43°F) to 37°C(99°F).

The south-west monsoon winds bring the rains from the end of June to the end of September. Sometimes the villagers have too little rain and sometimes too much, and it is not difficult to realise that both too little and too much rain cause hardship and loss of money when trying to cultivate crops.

Nimish and Nina might take you down to the two wells in the village where sweet drinking water can be drawn up. These wells are built in the bed of the river, and there is a pathway for fetching the water from the wells which is steep, so cement footsteps have been built for the villagers to carry the water more easily.

The hills surrounding the village are covered with different kinds of trees, and in the village itself there are about fifty trees that give shade to the villagers. Some of the trees are in the school playground and some on both sides of the National Highway.

Narinder could tell you that at one time there were many wild animals in the hills—leopards, pigs, deer, wolves, jackals and rabbits—but there are not so many now. Some of the birds you recognise quite easily, like sparrows, doves and parrots.

In the past the village had no regular roads connecting it with the other villages around. Bullock carts were the only means of transport, but with the building of the National Highway, State buses pass through the village and villagers are now able to go from one village to another more quickly. Goods, too, are carried by lorries and trucks, and so trade is helped. Crops are grown and articles made which are sold to other villages, so bringing more money into the family.

About three-quarters of the buildings are used for homes and a quarter for shops, workshops, schools and places where the whole community can meet to get to know each other and entertain or be entertained.

The houses are made in two different ways. One way is called **kutcha** and the other **pucca.** A kutcha house is made of stone, bamboo, mud and straw, and a pucca one of stones and bricks painted or plastered with

A house

cement or lime.

The most important material and the most commonly used in building houses is stone and this can be found in plenty in the stone quarries near the village. There are two kinds of stone, the rough stone and the slab stone.

The roofs of all the houses are generally double sloped to allow rainwater to flow down, and are covered with tiles which are turned before the monsoon to avoid the water leaking through into the house.

ed KUTCHA house

There are three types of houses, occupied by the very poor, the not-so-poor and the rich. The house of the very poor has its walls plastered with mud and roof covered with tiles or thatched with grass, and there is an open verandah with a kitchen and washstand in one corner. It has poor ventilation and is used throughout the day for anything that needs to be done; it is used as a living room, as a cattle shed and as a bedroom which men and women share.

The somewhat better house is made with stones and mud and is a kutcha house and there is a big entrance, without doors in the middle. The washstand and the kitchen are in the verandah with two rooms attached, one room used as a living room and a bedroom and the other as a store.

PUCCA house

The rich man's house has a big gate leading to an open space where a modern type of building has been erected. The walls of the house are built of stone and plastered with cement and lime; this pucca house is roomy and well-ventilated and has a bathroom and toilet. The other types of houses have no bathrooms or toilets.

The rich man's house has a separate space for keeping tools, and his bullocks are kept in

the front courtyard or near the outside verandah. Some of the other types of houses have small lofts where things that are not needed immediately are placed. Those houses have separate sleeping arrangements for married and unmarried members.

The richer people are able to buy furniture and household articles like a carpet, stool, wall-clock, record-player and radio, but these are luxuries for those with money; the poorer people are not able to buy any luxuries until they have food, clothing and a home.

The poorer Indians do not possess a stove, but in many houses their small tin or earthen bowl lamps are being replaced by hurricane lamps.

The richer people keep their cooked food in cupboards now, but in the poorer homes they have no cupboards. However, conditions in India are improving slowly and many changes in village life are taking place each year, but these changes are not fast enough for many Indians, and they are faced with the problem of staying where they are, in poor conditions, or of going to other places in the world, such as Britain, where they know they can earn more money and live more easily in better conditions.

The Shah family had to face this problem and decide what they were going to do. We will now see what happened when they made their decision.

THE JOURNEY TO BRITAIN

"Namaste!"

With this greeting Narinder Shah's next door neighbour folded his hands together and then said, "Where are you going, my friend?"

"I'm going with my family to Britain. My brother's there and he says there are many jobs for me to choose," said Narinder.

"But," said his neighbour, "Why don't you stay here in Baroda in this fine Gujarat State? There's work for you to do in India. I've a good job, and I'm sure you'll get a better one soon."

"No," said Narinder, "my family and I can't settle down here. Since we moved from the north-west of India, we've felt lost and there is so little farmland for all who want it that we feel we'll have a better life in Britain."

Narinder, Lalita, his wife, and their two children, Nimish and Nina had lived a few years in this village outside Baroda in the Gujarat State north of Bombay, and, although they had tried hard, they could see no future for themselves in India and were now willing to risk leaving their homeland for another country—Britain.

Their friends, who had left India, had told them about the many opportunities to earn money in Britain; more money than they could possibly hope to earn in their own village where goods were very cheap to buy, but wages were very low.

Narinder and Lalita wanted to live a better life with a better standard of living. They also wanted to work hard to get a better job and so earn more money to buy whatever they needed for the family. They did not mind if they had to work at night-school to learn a trade or to pass examinations. They did not mind, either, giving up some of their customs and traditions.

The decision to leave India had been taken, and Narinder and his family prepared to pack the few belongings they wished to take with them to Britain. They were only allowed forty-four pounds in weight per person on the aeroplane, so they had to decide on the most important and useful belongings they had.

Nimish and Nina found it difficult to leave any of their possessions behind and more difficult still to decide which things should be taken with them to Britain. However, with their mother's and father's help, everything was soon packed and ready to go.

Narinder had to find out about the times of the aeroplanes that flew to London Airport, so Nimish, Nina and he went to the Travel Agency and there they were given all the information they needed and were allowed to ask as many questions as they liked.

They discovered that there were four main air routes by which Indians travelled to London:

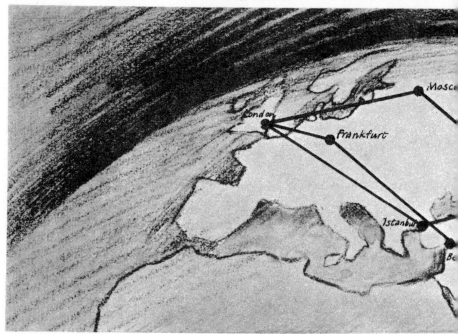

THE JOURNEY TO BRITAIN

1. **KUWAIT AIRWAYS** – from Bombay via Bahrain, Kuwait, Beirut, and Frankfurt to London.

2. **MIDDLE EAST AIRLINES** – from New Delhi to Bombay by Indian Airlines Corporation; from Bombay via Beirut to London.

3. **AIR INDIA** – from New Delhi via Moscow to London.

4. **B.O.A.C.** – from New Delhi via Teheran, Istanbul to London.

Narinder decided that they would fly from Bombay by Kuwait Airways. The fare would cost about £160 for the Economy Class single fare for each adult with a reduction in price for the children. In Rupees, the cost for each adult would be approximately 3,300 Rupees. Indians are allowed to take a maximum of £3 only out of India.

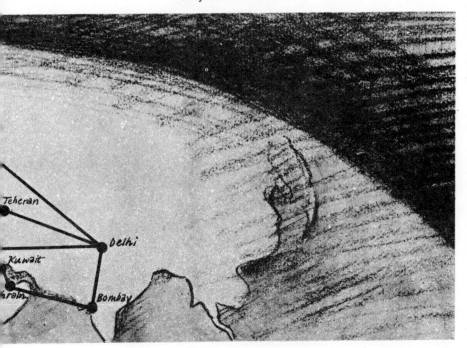

THE JOURNEY TO BRITAIN

The journey by aeroplane would be fast and comfortable and the time taken to reach London Airport (Heathrow) would be about twenty-five hours. Passengers are allowed to break their journey if they wish, but most Indians want to be in Britain as quickly as possible, so they travel with as little delay as is necessary. The Shah family decided not to delay.

Each person had to have a passport, health certificate and some money, as well as a small cabin-bag carrying anything that was needed for the journey, so Narinder made all these necessary arrangements.

At last everything was ready and they made their way to Bombay Airport. Nimish and Nina could not help asking questions all the time. What would the Airport be like? What would it feel like to leave the ground in an aeroplane? Would they feel ill? Would there be many other families like them going to Britain? What would it be like in London?

Narinder and Lalita were feeling just as excited as the children and found it difficult to answer all their questions; they did not know all the answers; it was a matter of waiting and seeing. But they were also feeling sad at the thought of leaving the older members of their family, their friends and their country; but they looked forward to a better time in Britain, to a time when they would be able to send money back to help at home and perhaps even to return to India some day, if only for a holiday.

They boarded the aeroplane; it was large and comfortable and they felt at home almost immediately. The air hostesses were busy seeing that everyone was happy and that they had all they wanted. Their journey had begun and the children snuggled down in their seats with their eyes fixed on the window.

It seemed to happen without their knowing it; they were in the air and climbing fast into the clouds; a new world was opening up to them. They seemed to be in a dream. Then the air hostess shattered their thoughts as she asked if they would like something to eat or drink -- some nuts or orange juice? Later they could have an evening meal and in the morning, breakfast.

The journey passed quickly. They had cruised at 25,000 ft., at an air speed of 580 miles per hour and had flown over desert country as well as having seen beautiful snow-capped mountain ranges.

Soon they were being told by the pilot that they were over the English Channel. This was followed by the order to fasten their safety belts, because the weather might be rough over the Channel and also they would soon be landing at London Airport .

As they came down, they felt deaf, but quickly recovered as they collected their cabin-bags and passed through the Customs and the Immigration Office.

Some Indian friends were waiting for them, and they were soon on their way to a home in London where they would meet other Indians from Gujarat, and where they would stay until they had a home of their own. One thing they did feel was the cold.

A SUGGESTIONS AND QUESTIONS

These are not questions you **have** to answer and the suggestions are not things you **have** to do. Choose something in which you are really interested and do your best to enjoy what you have chosen.

Things to Find Out

When Hindus arrive in Britain, they feel the cold. Find out about the weather in India at different times of the year and in different parts of India. What effect does the Indian weather have on Indians? What kind of clothes would **you** need to wear if you lived in India?

Things to Plan

Plan a journey to Bombay and think of all the things you would need for that journey and for a month's stay in India. Write to an Airline Corporation for particulars of the flight and speak to someone who has lived in India for a long time. He will be able to help you decide what you need and what you can do and see in India.

Things to Make

a. From pictures, and the description in this book, construct an Indian village. Make sure you use the correct materials to build the three different types of houses described on page 17.

b. Make collage pictures of different kinds of British houses.

c. Make a classbook about India. You can collect pictures of India from magazines, newspapers, airline posters and travel brochures.

Books to Read

Look at the pictures in a book called "India" by Richard Lannoy, Publisher: Thames and Hudson. Discuss in a small group what you see in a particular picture, and so learn more about India and the Indian way of living. If you do not know what a certain picture is about, you can turn to the end of the book where a description of the picture is given. There are other books about India which you will need if you are going to work in groups. Perhaps these will be in your school or class library.

From what you have read so far, make up some questions of your own, perhaps with the help of your teacher, and try to discover the answers through your parents, your teachers, and your library books.

7 HINDU RELIGION

In the Shah's village in Baroda, the people were very religious-minded. People of different faiths had their different temples and places of worship and some, on special occasions, used to fast for about a week, others used to fast every other day. There were special services where the Hindu scriptures were read and days when some of the village people would greet each other and ask for forgiveness for any injury or unkindness that had been done in the past year. Some of the village people worshipped the Sun and others, like Narinder and his family, worshipped the Hindu gods like **Shiva, Rama, Krishna** and others.

But in Britain, Narinder and Lalita found things very different. They soon realised they were in a country where Jesus Christ had been worshipped in cathedrals, churches and village halls for centuries and where there were no Hindu customs and temples; but they realised too that Britain was a free country where men and women worshipped, or did not worship, as they pleased; that people were not forced to worship in the Christian way, and that as Hindus they could worship in a hall which they could hire, or they could save enough money to build a temple, or larger place of worship. So Narinder and his friends hired a hall from a local Church on Sunday afternoons.

Each week they sing their Hindu hymns and have their scriptures read to them. They chant their prayers and have devotional songs, the soloist playing an Indian musical instrument and singing beautifully.

The atmosphere in the service is informal and the smaller children run about and talk occasionally in their high-pitched voices, but

no one minds as long as they do not make a loud noise and disturb the main flow of the service.

Sometimes there is a visiting speaker – a **swami** or religious instructor from India – a man of distinction who is a **mahatma** from northern India. There he spends much of his time meditating, or thinking, about God, in his mountain retreat, 12,000 feet up in the Himalaya mountains.

At the service in Britain he wears salmon-pink robes and a cap to match. His face shows strength of character and on his hooked nose he wears gold-rimmed spectacles. A gold watch is on his wrist.

He is able to speak English, but speaks Hindi at the service. He hugs his friends, but behaves in a cheerful and dignified way, and when the time comes for him to speak he sits cross-legged on a table and stresses the need for human beings to be decent to each other. "I give you my blessing, my hearty blessing," he says.

Often the Hindus think about the changes that are taking place in their religion in Britain. For instance many Hindus have begun eating beef which their religion would not allow them to eat in India; other Hindus are not going to the services and festivals; others do not keep in their homes the statues of gods and goddesses, which they worshipped in India .They do not say **puja** (prayer) by chanting religious verses, singing hymns, offering incense and lighting lamps. In England some Hindus pray morning and evening, others morning only, and others not at all.

What kind of thoughts do Narinder and

Lalita teach their own children, Nimish and Nina? What kind of teaching do Hindu children get in the rooms off the Hall on a Sunday afternoon?

Narinder tells his son and daughter that **Hinduism** is the oldest religion in the world, and that it has no single person, like Jesus Christ, whose message is written down in a book like the Bible.

Hinduism is rather like a river which has many streams feeding it; each stream adds something of human thoughts and actions which come from God and joins the other streams until all meet, having flowed through human life and returned to God.

Hinduism is not just a religion; it is more; it is a way of life. What matters most to Hindus is behaviour, and that is why when you meet a Hindu man or woman he is most polite and friendly and will do anything to make you happy and comfortable. He will not only give the best of his food and drink, but also see that you have as much as you want.

A Hindu feels he is free to live as he likes as long as he tries to seek the truth in all things and causes no injury to anyone in thought, word, or deed.

BRAHMA the Creator

The ancient name of this teaching was not "Hinduism." The River Sindhu which formed the border between India and Persia was called "Hindu" by the Persians and "Hindus" or "Indus" by the Greeks; and the people who lived beyond the river were given the same name.

The Hindus, however, do not mind where their religion began, because they do not believe that names, forms of religion and Churches are important; what is important to

VISHNU
the Preserver

them is the way that leads men, women and children to noble thoughts and actions, which they believe finally lead them to God.

Now let us imagine that I am talking to Nimish and I want to know more about his beliefs as they have been taught him by his parents.

My question: "Nimish, what do you think about God?"

Nimish: "I believe God is everywhere and that God is not male or female. God is as much She, the Mother of the Universe, as He, the Father of the Universe. The word for God is 'Brahman' which is neuter, neither male nor female, but the Hindus have a special name for God as the Jews have when they use the word Yahweh. Our name for God is **Om** or **Aum**, the One Supreme Being."

My question: "What, then, does **Aum** look like?"

Nimish: "I cannot answer this question easily, because no one has seen **Aum**. He has no form or shape, but we believe he may take a form and come to earth at any time, at any place and on any planet."

My question: "Is that why you have many names of different gods and goddesses?"

Nimish: "Yes, these gods and goddesses are part of **Aum**. There are **Brahma**, the Creator, **Vishnu** the Preserver, **Shiva** the Destroyer, and **Shakti** the Mother Goddess who has many forms. There are also many others."

My question: "How was the world created?"

Nimish: "Hindus believe, and have believed for thousands of years, that the Universe is not just our planet but that countless other worlds exist, and that this is not the first time

SHIVA
the Destroyer

that God has created the world. He created and dissolved, creates and dissolves and will create and dissolve the worlds as well as individual bodies.

"You will be interested to know that a daily prayer chanted by Hindus for thousands of years has these words:

'O God, You created the sun, the moon, and the earth as you had created them before.......' "

My question: "What do you think about the soul of man?"

Nimish: "I believe that the soul of man is a spark of God and that it is never born and will never die. Someone has said that the spirit or soul is like a man who changes his clothes and so the spirit changes its bodies. The body may be young or old, ill or dead, but the spirit inside it cannot die. When the body dies, the same person, the same spirit is born again as another child elsewhere.

"Hindus believe that they get new bodies according to their previous life. For example, if they have hurt someone with their hand, they may be born in the next life with a withered hand. The Hindus have a word for this: it is the word **Karma** and may remind you of your Christian Bible: 'Whatever a man sows, that he will also reap.' "

My question: "Nimish, I have heard of yoga. What does it mean and has it anything to do with your religion?"

Nimish: "Yes, it has a very important part to play in our religion; some people would say it is the highest and most important part of the Hindu religion.

"**Yoga** is a Sanskrit word and it means 'being one with God' or 'having union with

God.' Everyone can have this union with God and even if they do not unite themselves with God in this life, Hindus believe they will have many more life-times in which they can do this."

My question: "But how do you get this union with God?"

Nimish: "It is difficult to tell you in detail, but very simply prayer and worship help you to get nearer God, and also the way you live trying to get rid of any unkind or unclean thought, word or deed. Hindus believe you may discover the way for yourself, or be helped by a guru who will teach you the way to freedom from sorrow and suffering, doubt and want."

My question: "What are the Hindu Scriptures?"

Nimish: "The most important Scriptures are called the **Vedas**. The word 'Veda' comes from the Sanskrit meaning 'knowledge.' There are four Vedas and Hindus believe that they were given to the first four human beings. There are twenty thousand hymns in the books and a knowledge of these is handed down from family to family. They are so old that no-one knows the exact date when they were written, but they are written in a very ancient form of Sanskrit."

My question: "What are the other Scriptures?"

Nimish: "There are many other Scriptures written in a later form of Sanskrit and these are probably more popular than the four Vedas. The most important is the **Bhagavad Gita** which means 'the Song of God', and this was the teaching given by Lord Krishna to Arjuna, the Warrior Prince."

KRISHNA

HINDU RELIGION   31

My question: "Can you let me see some favourite lines from the Vedas and from 'the Song of God?'"

Nimish: "Yes, certainly. But first I will let you see them in Sanskrit.

These words are repeated every morning by millions of Indians: 'Tat Savitur Vareniam Bhargo Devasya Dhimahi Dhiyo Yo Nah Pracodayat.'

"This means: 'Let our meditation be on the glorious light of Savitri, may this light illumine our minds.'

"The second is from 'The Song of God': 'We praise Thee with our thoughts, O God. We praise Thee even as the sun praises Thee in the morning: may we find joy in being Thy servants. Keep us under Thy protection. Forgive our sins and give us Thy love.'"

My question: "Will you tell me something about the Hindu Festivals that are held in England?"

Nimish: "Yes, I should love to, but I think Nina is longing to tell you something. We all go to the festivals as a family and enjoy them very much, so Nina will know as much about them as I.

"Come on, Nina, tell us what you know about our festivals in England."

Nina: "Thank you, Nimish. I have been wanting to say something for quite a time. I like our festivals very much, they're great fun. I have tried to find out all I can about them and Mummy and Daddy have helped me to understand them as much as I am able.

"There are many festivals held in India; some are important to a village only, others are of importance to Hindus all over India. India is a land of celebrations and some festival is always being held somewhere, for

Indians love to share their food and meet people, as well as sing, dance and play musical instruments.

"So it is quite natural that when Indians come over to England they do not want to forget their happy times, but want to remember them by coming together whenever and wherever they can, and that is a reason why we enjoy the British festivals such as Christmas, and celebrate in many ways like British people.

"Sometimes a festival celebrates one season coming to an end and another one beginning – the old is dying, a new season is being born: **Divali, the Festival of Lights** is at the end of October which is the end of autumn and the beginning of winter. The festival day for the renewal of vows is at the end of the dry season in India and at the beginning of the Monsoon. **Holi**, the festival of colours, is held at the end of winter and the beginning of spring in March. The Hindu New Year falls between March and April for the same reason. The festival of good over evil lasts from September to October."

My Question: "Can you tell me more about Divali? It sounds very interesting."

Nina: "Yes, indeed. Divali is a red-letter day in the Hindu Calendar. It is the one day which every Indian whose way of life began in old Hindustan celebrates. Not only Hindus, but Sikhs, Jains and Buddhists from Kashmir in the north of India to Cape Kumaran in the south join in happy friendship and remember something that happened a very long time ago."

This is the story as Nina told me.

H.F.B.—C

RAMA

"Thousands of years ago there lived a good King called **Rama** who was born into a noble fighting caste and who married a lovely girl called **Sita**. Some years after, there was a bitter quarrel in the royal family. In order to honour two promises of his father, **King Dasratha**, and as commanded by his step-mother, Rama decided to go into exile for fourteen years to live as a hermit in the forest. His faithful wife and his loyal brother, **Luxmana**, went with him.

"One day, while Rama was hunting the golden deer and his brother was out in search of him, Sita was sitting alone in their cottage. Suddenly, she was startled by an intruder. It was **Ravana**, the powerful demon-king from Ceylon. She had no hope of escaping from him and he forced her to travel with him to Ceylon, which was called Lanka.

"On hearing what had happened to his Queen from the birds whom he befriended, the sad King, together with his brother, followed as quickly as they could travel.

"They gained the willing help of the tribes along their way and after a long and perilous journey in which they endured many hardships they finally reached the coast opposite Lanka.

"With the aid of a local tribe, who threw rocks into the water and so built a bridge, they crossed into Lanka with their 'army of righteousness,' many years after the Queen had been captured by the Demon-King, Ravana.

"Rama and his army fought many battles and destroyed most of Ravana's Kingdom. At the same time he was able to rescue his captive Queen who remained as beautiful as she had always been, even though she had missed her husband and had wanted to return to him.

"King and Queen returned to their own Kingdom and their people welcomed them back as they had never welcomed anyone before. The people shouted and cheered at their return and asked the King to rule over them again. So from that day onward the occasion is remembered as a time when good overcame evil, and when light triumphed over darkness."

Nina continued: "Divali is a family festival when family vows are renewed: the husband remembers his duty to his wife and the wife to her husband; the elder brother to the younger brother; the father to his son and the son to his father. Boys are told to be like King Rama and girls like Queen Sita. It is a special time for us as children, for at this time even the poorest parents give us toys and new clothes."

My question: "What does 'Divali' mean?"

Nimish: "I can answer that for you.

"The word 'Divali' comes from an ancient word 'deep-avali' or 'festival of Lights' and the day is the end to the previous 'Nava-ratrai' (nine nights) festivities which begin at the end of September and which are observed all over India under different names.

"For some Hindus Divali is also a New Year; for others a huge figure, or effigy of Ravana, the Demon-King, is built and then burnt as fireworks are lit. Fireworks and crackers play an important part in the celebration of Divali and it is a time when we young especially enjoy ourselves.

"At this time, traders open new account books and light up their shops. Everyone is supposed to wear new clothes and gifts are exchanged. Women put marigolds and sweet-smelling jasmine in their hair. Craftsmen dedicate their tools and everyone joins in the worship of Luxuri, the goddess of luxury. For up to three nights, especially the night before, rows upon rows of lights are seen everywhere – mustard-oil lamps in the villages and electric lights in the cities; some parts of Bombay look just like your famous Blackpool illuminations at this time.

"Divali is celebrated all over the world wherever the people of India are gathered. In Britain the different Indian clubs, associations and communities keep the occasion on different dates, according to how convenient it is to meet together.

"Here in Britain we have all kinds of difficulties – a strange climate, strange food, strange customs and strange people around them. But our guru or priest will remind us that we must be like Rama, the Bright Shining One, and follow his example by overcoming the difficulties, by winning friends and allies, and by so doing we will defeat the present-day 'Ravana' of ignorant darkness and evil, and so will be able to live happier lives."

My question: "Thank you for helping me to understand about Hindu festivals and especially Divali, but will you take me to a Divali meeting so that I can see for myself what happens?"

Nina: "Certainly. Everyone is welcome to come along at the Hindu Centre in London and you may come with your family. I will arrange to meet you outside the Church Hall in the centre of the town. We meet there

every Sunday, and hold our services and
meetings there, until we have saved up
enough money to buy land and a building of
our own."

Divali: A Hindu Festival.

8

A HINDU FESTIVAL

I met the Shah family at 3.45 p.m. on Sunday, 29th October, the day they were celebrating Divali. It was a wet day but this did not prevent hundreds of cars travelling up and down the main street causing traffic jams and making it difficult for pedestrians to cross the road.

As I waited for the Shah family in the entrance of the Hall, I noticed some people were walking up to the Hall, while others came by car, mostly in Minis or Morris 1100's. The Hindu men were dressed in their best suits, as I was dressed in mine, and some of the Hindu women wore saris, while others were dressed in skirts and blouses like British women.

The Shah family greeted me with smiles and Narinder Shah said that he was pleased to see me and hoped that I would enjoy this family festival.

I was taken to the front rows of seats where I discovered guests were taken. These seats were seats of honour and I appreciated being in them. Other guests were there too, both British and Indian. Often Indian guests are people of high social position in India, and together with their British friends are welcomed personally and have their names read out to all those present in the Hall. The Indians were asked to stand. They did so and folded their hands together in greeting.

We sat down and I looked around. The Hall was filling up fast and before 4 p.m. men and women were having to stand at the sides of the Hall. There were no more empty seats: they did not want to miss the festivities.

It was, as Nina had said, a family occasion when grandmother, grandfather, mother, father and children came to be together and talk even while the various items were in progress.

To enable the older people to sit down on seats the children were provided with large woollen mats which were placed on the floor in front of the apron of the stage. There they sat and knelt, or if they were small enough stood so that their eyes were just above the apron edge.

Most of the Indian children were dressed as you would see English children dressed – the girls in short skirts and coloured jumpers; the boys in anoraks and short trousers or in suits with long trousers. One or two girls were dressed in **saris**: they were the exception, but they looked very attractive with their dark hair and very appealing eyes.

The children clapped and responded to everything that was performed and were not very keen when mother called for them to leave in the middle of a performance.

The adults sat row upon row in seats on either side of a not very wide aisle, men and women together. In the middle of the festivities when the Hall was very crowded with about five hundred people, many of them standing, the President of the Hindu Centre in London interrupted the entertainment by coming to the microphone to ask the men to give up their seats to the women who had come in late. There was an immediate response and all the women were given seats within a few moments.

A number of Indian men had brought along their cameras with electronic flash or with flash bulbs. They darted about the front of the Hall trying hard not to get in the way of anyone's view of the performers, but wanting very much to find the right position to take the best photograph of the artist or artists on the stage.

On the apron of the stage were two lighted candles, one on each side, reminding the audience that this performance was connected with the 'Festival of Lights', Divali, the triumph of good over evil.

The programme was varied and interesting and visitors were invited to bring their friends along with them. Admission was free, there were light refreshments and a gift of Indian sweets for everyone present.

When all the arrangements were completed, when the audience were in their seats, the microphone on the stage, the backstage hands and the artists ready, the President of the Hindu Centre in London walked up to the microphone and chanted in Sanskrit a hymn of praise to Lord Rama and introduced in Hindi the festival of devotion and love, Divali.

The President then spoke in English a word of welcome to distinguished guests from India, as well as to the English visitors. He followed this welcome by explaining in Hindi the story of Lord Rama.

The scene was now set for the items of entertainment. First there was a scene in India where the ladies and girls were dancing: the women were dressed in saris with sequins of different colours – red, yellow, pink and black, and they danced gracefully over the stage clapping their hands to a background of Indian music.

Next followed another scene in India where a leader of the local community was being interviewed by another woman and a member of the Press who asked why he was doing nothing about the poor conditions in the area. This discussion was spoken in Hindi.

Songs and dances made up the remainder of the programme. For one song a musical instrument called a sitar was used, for another a small harmonium. For the dances a young Indian girl, dressed in a green sari with a red and gold sash diagonally across her body with thick bangles on her ankles and thin ones on her wrist, interpreted an Indian mythological story in a most expressive and beautiful dance. The movements of her eyes, head, hands, feet and body seemed to speak to the audience as she danced with a long tress of black hair flowing down her back.

At the interval announcements were given in Hindi and English apologising for the lack of accommodation and appealing for money to build a larger building. Gifts were accepted there and then, and varied from a £1 to a penny given by a small girl dressed in a sari. More dances and songs followed as well as recitations in Hindi by Hindu children. The festivities ended three hours after they had started.

9 **DEATH**

"BOXER DIES AFTER FIGHT WIN."
"AIRLINE CRASH: 98 KILLED."
"THE PRICE OF FISH: 152 DEATHS IN
17 YEARS."
"EARTHQUAKE DISASTER –
400 FEARED DEAD."

Newspapers and television never stop reminding us of some loss of life in some part of the world. Often the news goes in one ear and out of the other, but a death in a family or in a school is different.

Sometimes at the bottom of a garden there is a small wooden cross stuck in the earth. It is the grave of a child's pet, perhaps a rabbit, a hamster, or a budgerigar. The pet has died, a hole has been dug and the dead body, wrapped in an old newspaper, is placed in the hole and covered with earth and leaves. A cross, made out of twigs or broken parts of an old wooden box, is placed carefully in the earth over the dead body. It is a sad event.

As we get older we take the death of animal for granted, but we feel differently when death strikes a person near to us. Some have lost a mother or father; others one or more grandparents; some of us a friend of the family; and this leads us to ask questions, for we feel curious about death: "What really happens when we die?" "Do we live again?" "Is there life after death?"

We know too that everyone will die at some time or other and that some people will meet death early in life and others not until they are ninety or a hundred years old. Every year medical science helps people to live longer and in some cases hearts are transplanted from a dead body to a person who has a chance of living if he is given another heart to replace his own.

As we discover all these things, we also discover that although we have lost someone whom we have known and loved, we still have other people who love us and who are willing to help us. Christians believe that this is one of God's ways of showing that He always loves us and that He is always present with us. He shows His love through people who love us, as well as in other ways.

The person who has died is in some sense still with us, because we know of that person's ideas and hopes, of his sense of values, and of his intentions, and as long as these things are part of us, we keep alive his way of living and thinking.

Sometimes the death of one person brings out new life in another person. For instance, if a family lose the mother through death, and the daughter has to take on the responsibility of the home; she has to plan and prepare the meals, see that the rest of the family look clean and tidy, and arrange the running of the home as the mother did. This is the way life goes on, and it is also one way in which life comes out of death.

Some of the people who love us do not know what to say to us about death, because they are puzzled and perplexed, some believe there is nothing more after death.

Christians believe that God's love and presence surround us all the time and that although the dead body does not move of itself, and cannot do the things that our live bodies can do, life has not ended and the real person, the soul or spirit of man, is still living and is still surrounded by God's love.

Christians believe God is with them in life and death, because they believe in the life, death and resurrection of Jesus Christ, and that one day they will be given a new body quite unlike their present one.

Christians will tell you that the person who has died is not really dead. Only his body is dead, but the real person who lived in the body is alive somewhere else. This is difficult to understand and no-one can prove this, but we do know that if we take a seed and put it in the ground it looks rather dead. We also know that the flower or the fruit that eventually appear do not look at all like the seed, though one comes from the other. So it could be that the life in the body does at some stage have a new body unlike the present one and quite beyond our imagination.

The Hindus have an idea similar to this. Some Hindu people believe that the soul is the spark of God. Others believe that the soul is independent of God and exists as something that is separate from God and from the body.

In either way of thinking the soul was never born and will never die. All Hindus believe that when the body dies the same person, the same soul or spirit is born again as another child in another place on earth. This is called the transmigration of the soul.

Hindus believe that the soul or spirit of man continues for all time: "As a man changes his clothes, so the spirit changes its bodies. The body is young, or old, or sick, or withered or dead; but the spirit within cannot die."

Hindus believe that the new bodies they get depend on what they have done in their previous life. If they have been good, then they will have whole bodies; if they have not, then they will have some defect, such as being blind, or deaf, or dumb.

So it is important for a Hindu to think carefully about how he should live and speak. We have already learnt that there is a verse in the Christian Bible that says: "Whatever a man sows, that he will also reap." The Hindus try to remember this, so that as the soul goes from body to body it becomes purer and purer until in the end it reaches God.

In India thousands of Hindus visit the holy river **Ganges**. They believe that if they bathe in its waters they are made pure. Along the banks of the river stands the city of Benares where many Hindus wish to have their ashes scattered after they have died and been cremated.

Along the banks of the river are stone steps on which the dead bodies are placed for cremation. These steps are called **ghats** and it is on the ghats that the bodies are burned before the ashes are scattered.

The news about the death is told to the relatives and friends immediately. Telegrams are sent to all the closest relatives who happen to be away from the town or village and the dead body is not moved until the nearest relatives have arrived within twelve or fifteen hours after the death.

The dead body is washed and made clean before it is wrapped and put in the coffin and then placed on a bier or movable stand.

The bier is carried on the shoulders of six relatives while the other relatives, friends and neighbours follow the coffin silently towards the cremation ground. The dead body is placed on a pyre or pile of wood and covered with small pieces of dry wood and sandal wood. **Ghee**, a kind of butter, is also thrown on the pyre to help the fire catch alight easily. Dry pieces of squeezed sugar cane are lit and placed on different sides of the pyre, and hymns from the Hindu sacred books are chanted by the priest. No one is expected to leave until the body is no longer to be seen. The mourners are then led out of the cremation ground, thanks are given to those who have attended the funeral and everyone leaves for home.

The next day the bereaved family come together and visit the cremation ground to collect the bones and ashes which are then immersed in the holy waters of the Ganges.

On the fourth day the relatives and friends again visit the house of the dead person to express their grief and to comfort the family. A ceremony is held, and money, food and clothes are given as gifts to the bereaved family, and prayers are offered for the peace of the departed soul.

On the eleventh or sometimes the thirteenth day after the death, the **Kriya** ceremony is performed. This is the last ceremony, and once again all those who were mourners earlier, and others who could not come before, meet to sympathise with the family.

At the cremation ceremony the Indian priest recites the following from the **Gita: "The Song of God"**

"Know this Atman (Soul)
Unborn, undying,
Never ceasing,
Never beginning,

DEATH

Deathless, birthless,
Unchanging for ever
How can it die
The death of the body?

Knowing it birthless,
Knowing it deathless,
Knowing it endless,
For ever unchanging,
Dream not you do
The deed of the killer,
Dream not the power
Is yours to command it.

Worn out garments
Are shed by the body,
Worn-out bodies
Are shed by the dweller
Within the body,
New bodies are donned
By the dweller, like garments.

Not wounded by weapons,
Not burned by fire,
Not dried by the wind,
Not wetted by water,
Such is the Atman (Soul).

Not dried, not wetted,
Not burned, not wounded,
Innermost element,
Everywhere, always,
Being of beings,
Changeless, eternal
For ever and ever."

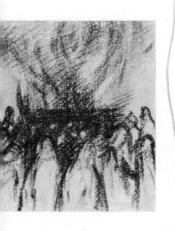

To help the relatives of the dead person, the
truth is impressed upon them that the real

self, the soul, is not dead, because it can never die. The priests may say words like these: "You ought not to be sorry. Death is certain for the born. Re-birth is certain for the dead. You should not grieve for what is unavoidable.

"Before birth beings are not shown to our human senses; between birth and death they are seen; at death they return unseen again. What is there in all this to grieve over?

"He who dwells within all living bodies remains for ever indestructible. Therefore you should never mourn for anyone."

In Britain, too, Hindus are cremated; only here their dead bodies are taken to a Crematorium and a short ceremony takes place with the whole family present. Hindus believe that the body comes from ashes and goes back into ashes.

Some of the words heard in the cremation ceremony are these:

"May your eyesight return to the sun, your breath to the winds, may your waters mingle with the ocean and your earthly part become one with the earth."

And at the end of the ceremony, as at the end of all Hindu ceremonies, these words are said:

"Peace be in the higher worlds, peace be in the firmament, peace be on earth. May the waters flow peacefully, may the herbs and shrubs grow peacefully, may all the divine powers bring unto us peace. Brahman, the Supreme, is peace. May all be in peace, in peace and only in peace, and may that peace come unto me. Aum, Peace, Peace, Peace."

INDIAN DANCING

When the Shah family go to a festival like Divali or to some form of entertainment such as a film or a concert, they enjoy watching the Indian girls dancing. The girls' movements are very beautiful and expressive and there is great feeling in their performance.

Nina especially is very interested, as she would like to be a good dancer, and at Divali she was able to see a dancer who, after winning national dancing diplomas, had travelled many hundreds of miles in India and had danced before many hundreds of Indians.

Nina thought she would like to find out more about Indian dancing. She discovered that the art of dancing started in India hundreds of years before Christ, and that the Greeks learned dancing by gesture or movement of the hands from the Indians after Alexander the Great's invasion of India in 327 B.C.

Hindus believe that dancing is the most beautiful of all the arts and through their dancing they tell stories and legends about their Hindu gods, so that their religion can be understood better.

There is a Hindu legend that the world was created in a dance when Brahma, the Creator, took three great strides: his downward stride made the earth, space appeared with his next stride, and the sky appeared with the third stride.

Tradition says that dancing was handed down by the gods. The first dancer was said to be **Siva** the god (known, too, as Lord Shiva or Nataraja) and he was known as the king of dancers; but dancing is more likely to have started from the Hindus' ancestors who

INDIAN DANCING

worshipped nature and danced to please the gods.

At one time in their early history the Hindu priests were the only ones to be allowed to read the four Vedas or Holy Books of the Hindu religion. This was thought to be very unfair by the ordinary people of the community, the warriors, the traders and the workers, so they complained to Brahma.

Nina had read one of the old Indian stories about their gods and she had learnt that Brahma thought about their complaint for a while and then asked Indra, the king of the gods, to read a new book that he, Brahma, had written. It was entitled the 'Book of Knowledge and Drama.' Indra refused, so Brahma decided to let a wise man called Bharata Muni read it.

Bharata enjoyed reading the book and learned so much from it that he himself wrote a book on dancing, drama and music.

He gathered together dancers and musicians from all around him and gave his first performance in front of Lord Siva himself. Lord Siva was very pleased with what he saw and gave Bharata all the help he could to make his dancing perfect.

Lord Siva's wife taught him all the women's movements and another god taught him all the men's movements in dancing. Soon the whole art of dancing was passed from the gods to men on earth.

During the days of Buddha, dance drama was practised everywhere and, before the birth of Christ, Buddhist monks travelled to Japan and China taking with them their religion and the art of dancing.

At one time only female temple dancers

Lord of the Dance

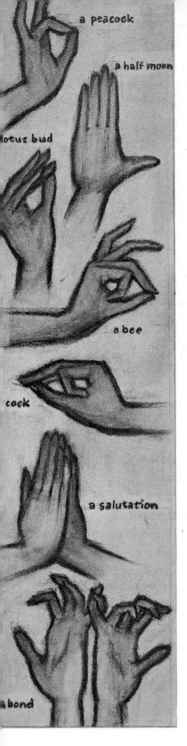

a peacock

a half moon

lotus bud

a bee

cock

a salutation

a bond

were allowed to perform these dances, but now Indian boys and girls can learn how to dance the Bharata Natyam dances. Nina is pleased about this and practises the dances in Britain.

If Nina wanted to dance seriously, she would have to learn many movements of the body. Each part of the body has a particular movement and a particular meaning – the head, hips, chest, neck, shoulders, stomach, back, thighs, elbows, knees, ankles, lips, teeth, mouth, tongue, nose, cheek and eyes all speak to the audience according to the way they are moved.

The hands also are moved in a particular way. The Indians have a name for the gestures of the hands: it is **Hasta Mudra.** One gesture can mean "the wind" or "the abode of the gods" or "holding a sword" or "a year".

What matters most is the position of the hand and the way in which it is moved and a Hindu audience can interpret the meaning of the gesture when it sees the hand in a particular position.

The Hindu dance has strict rules and traditions. Brahmins must always have white faces, female demons must always wear black robes and blue stones, while goddesses must have green clothes and pearls.

Just as the audience can recognise different characters by the coloured clothes they wear, so also do they feel the mood of the dancer whether he is afraid, or happy, or angry, by the movement of the dancer's face.

In addition an atmosphere is created by the musicians who have various musical instruments such as cymbals, drums and sitars. One of the largest kinds of melon can

have its gourd or outer shell dried and be
made into a guitar or a saringha. The snake
charmer's pipe has a small hollow gourd
with two reeds stuck through it for the fingers
to play upon.

Indian music has a long tradition behind it
and has connections with Egyptian, Persian
and Arabic music. It is based on song, and
the many stringed and wind instruments show
how flexible the human voice can be.

Indian music perhaps sounds queer to
listen to, because Indian musicians make
use of many more notes than players in
Britain or Europe, but this helps the dancers.

As they watch the dances, Hindus enter
into the spirit of the dance, and as they do so
they feel closer to their gods.

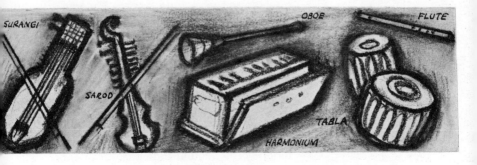

11 CASTE

The people in India are not conscious of colour distinctions as we are. People in the same family may be dark or nearly white and it is rare to see the same colour all through the family. There are not colour but caste distinctions.

Some Hindus believe that caste was given by God and that there are four kinds of people. One of their religious books says that at the beginning of the world "there were no Kings and no Kingdoms; all people ruled over themselves and over each other through a sense of virtue and duty." Spiritually they were all equal and they are known as the people of the pure and godly Swan caste.

But, as men and women began to take no notice of their duties, ideas about certain kinds of people were formed and they were divided into four divisions or castes.

The first were the thinkers or philosophers, the hermits and priests who gave their lives to the spiritual guidance and the education of the people. They are still devoted to the vow of poverty, so they must not have a lot of money nor anything that makes life comfortable. They must always try to live a life of truth, non-violence, love and wisdom.

The next were the people who helped to keep the law and ruled the people by good government, and, if necessary, became soldiers to fight off invaders.

The third were the people who were responsible for trade, industry, agriculture, and land-ownership. They were taxed heavily and if they did not spend most of their money on helping to build roads, hospitals or other public works, their wealth could be taken from them by the ancient Indian governments.

Because they were the richest, they were the lowest of the upper three castes.

And the last were the people who worked with their hands and all those who were unable to use their minds intelligently.

Often children who were born into one caste could rise to a higher group or descend to a lower group, according to what they made of their lives and according to their conduct.

The present caste system came from the ancient Hindu way of living. Slowly over the years people began to keep family secrets which they did not wish to pass on to others. Then came the Muslim victories in India when invaders came from Arabia, Persia and Turkey to try to destroy Indian civilisation. It was at this time that the Hindus survived by drawing themselves into close compartments or castes. Hindus think that each person is best fitted to a particular profession, for example, a doctor or a teacher, or to a particular type of life according to his temperament. They believe that before the age of five a child is influenced by his family and surroundings. The priests are mostly trained by their families and so ancient traditions are passed from one generation to another, but training colleges have now been built and some of them admit students from non-priestly castes as well.

It is important to remember that in present-day India to call anyone of low caste is against the law, and the person who does this can be punished. A great deal of time and money is being spent, so that everyone can enjoy modern education, social opportunities, and civil rights.

In Britain, the caste system is loosening

and does not work easily, because life is so different from India. Hindus work in the factories and eat together in the canteen, as well as meet and sit together when they worship. Wages are the same for the low and high castes and for the non-educated and the educated.

On the other hand, some individual Hindus have their friends in Britain only from the same caste and even form a savings club or a social club and do not allow members who are outside their own caste. Not many do this and not all members of the caste agree with this way of living.

Some craftsmen – carpenters, tailors, barbers and goldsmiths – earn extra money in their spare time by working for other Indians in the jobs for which they have been trained in India. The Brahmans, however, do not act as priests, as the Hindus have no temples here as the Sikhs have, because by Indian custom the complicated rituals are forbidden on foreign soil, and in Gujarat there is still a religious law against travelling across the sea. A hundred years ago travel abroad by a Hindu meant that he was made an outcaste, especially if he were a Brahman, and even now some castes insist on a special ritual when the Hindu returns to his own land.

Among those Hindus in Gujarat and the Punjab who are more western in their thinking, temple worship is growing to mean less and less, for to the Hindu religious life is based on personal belief and does not need a temple in which to worship.

The ritual duties of the Hindu immigrants are usually left to be done in India by a member of the family who is still living there.

This is true even for marriage and funeral rites, for these can be carried out in India by the family while a short ceremony is held in Britain.

Caste may not work in this country for the immigrant, but however long he may be away from the village-caste group in Gujarat or the Punjab, he does not lose his membership of it except by breaking one of its most important rules, such as marrying outside the caste, religion or region. Even then he may not be made an outcaste unless he breaks another rule important to the caste-group.

12 **LALITA THE HINDU MOTHER**

I expect when you have been away from home without mother, you may have felt a little homesick and wanted your own toys, games and books, perhaps your own room, or your own particular friend; you may have wished, too, that your mother had been with you to do all the jobs that you take for granted at home – the cooking, the washing and mending of clothes, the special treats for special occasions. You may have missed, above all, the love, care and thought that most mothers give to their children. You may even have remembered the odd telling-off and the cross word which you deserved!

I expect, too, that most of you have only been away from home for a short while – perhaps in hospital, or with an aunt or uncle while mother has not been well, or even on holiday without any of the other members of the family.

But I wonder if you can imagine what it is like to know that you may never be able to see your mother again, or that you may not see her for many years, and that you will have to save up a lot of money to travel many thousands of miles to her own village or town.

If you can imagine this, then you may be nearer to understanding what it is like for Hindu men and women like Narinder and Lalita who have left their own villages and towns where their parents live and have come to set up home in Britain. They cannot take a short journey by bus, car, or train to see their relatives and friends.

The role of the Hindu mother in Britain is different from the role of the Hindu mother in India. In Britain the Hindu mother likes to go to work to earn more money for the family, so

she gets up about seven o'clock in the morning, prepares the breakfast for the family and, if she has not already done so the night before, she prepares a picnic lunch for her husband and sometimes for her children, although most Indian children stay to school dinners. If her husband works at night, he may say that he will get his own meal after he has had a sleep and a rest. When the wife comes back from work, she prepares and clears away the evening meal.

The Hindu mother is respected by the Hindu father. Since Aum or God may be called She as well as He in Hindu thinking, women are regarded very highly. There are many goddesses as well as gods.

Every girl is called **Kanya Devi** which means the girl-goddess of the home. **Shrimati Shah Devi** is the married name of the mother of our Hindy family. **"Shrimati"** is the same as "Mrs." as **"Shri"** is the same as "Mr." **Devi** means "goddess:" every Hindu woman is referred to as a goddess and since **"Ji"** is a further term of respect she is also addressed as **"Deviji."**

Lalita, like all Hindu women, runs the home and controls it completely. The average Hindu man has no say in the home at all and does not help very much in the house, not even when his wife is at work.

Further, the Hindu wife is not given an allowance of money for food and clothes, as in most British families, rather it is the other way, the husband gets an allowance from his wife, because at the end of the week or month when the Hindu man is paid, he hands all his wages to his mother or wife, and she divides the money out and gives him what she can spare.

Throughout the ages, India has had many queens, women poets, women philosophers, women authors and women warriors. In some Indian villages the entire elected council consists only of women members, and no male candidate of any political party in India ever hopes to win an election against a woman candidate.

You may have heard of the word **purdah** which is the practice of keeping women behind closed doors. This practice started with the Muslims who at one time invaded India.

At that time women were not safe, and so the Muslims introduced this practice. In those parts of India where Muslims never ruled, purdah is unknown, and it is not followed in Britain, where Indian women and girls work in factories, on buses and trains and in shops. They also walk about the streets doing their shopping and visiting friends, as well as entertaining British and Indian guests at home.

13 LALITA IN THE KITCHEN

Indians admire and respect a woman who looks after the family well, does the shopping, cooks the meals on time, and still has time to enjoy her husband and children and join in the fun they have together.

Indian women enjoy cooking and not only buy food from shops owned by Indians, but also buy British food from the supermarkets. Like a British family, some of the Indian family like one thing, others like something else. Often Narinder and Lalita have more Indian food than Nimish and Nina. The children like to try British food, as they have school dinners and enjoy the food they eat in the school canteen.

Narinder and Lalita have been brought up like millions of other Hindus to be vegetarians. They do not like to eat anything that has hurt any kind of living creature, so that fish, eggs and meat are not eaten.

This may seem strange to you, but Indian Hindus, living in a poor country where millions are starving, prefer to die rather than kill an animal or bird or fish to eat. They believe that all life is one, although life has many forms, and some forms, such as human beings, have more developed parts (e.g. the hands and brain) than other creatures.

In Britain and in other more developed countries the Hindus have accepted the need to eat anything that is available in a British restaurant or café, but they usually prefer not to eat animal food at home. Their food is simple during the week, rice and pulse vegetables being important, but at the week-end they have large pieces of chicken in curry for those in the family, usually the children, who like meat.

The older members of the family enjoy vegetables, such as cauliflower, potatoes, greens, cabbage, peas, carrots and ladyfingers. Small ladyfingers are better for taste than large ones and have smaller seeds as well.

Hindus also like green chillies which have a hot taste, and yellow and red chillies which are very hot and cause a burning sensation in the throat when they are eaten.

For their cooking they use ghee, which is a kind of butter or fat made from cow's or buffalo's milk, and mustard oil which is made from mustard seeds crushed in machines.

The Shah family have for breakfast a cup of tea, some biscuits, a boiled egg and toast. They may also have cereals that British families enjoy: "Corn-flakes," "Ricicles," "Wheat flakes," "Shredded Wheat" and "Weetabix."

The children are often out for lunch at school, though father and mother often carry their lunch with them for eating at the factory. The main meal of the day is the evening meal and all the family are present.

But if some of the family are at home for lunch, then they have a vegetable curry – lentils with boiled rice and chapatti with butter. Afterwards they have butter-milk or yogurt. Their curry is always very tasty with hot spices and red chutney.

For tea, the family have a cup of tea with savoury snacks and biscuits, and for the evening meal they have curried chicken as well as savoury snacks. Narinder and Lalita have many vegetable and rice dishes, salads with hot pickles, home-made yogurt.

Food is important to Hindus for it provides a link with their homeland. In their homes the kitchen and the dining room are the most important rooms. After the kitchen and dining room the next most important room is the one for receiving visitors and after that the "sleeping space" or bedroom.

Sometimes the kitchen is large and there is no need for a separate dining room; when there is a dining room, it can be used to receive visitors or even as an extra bedroom. The kitchen always contains a mixture of Indian and British food and cooking utensils.

One day you might like to ask your mother to cook a Hindu meal similar to one eaten by the Shah family. You might like to try eating the food your mother cooks with your fingers and not with knives and forks, and then you would be copying Nimish and Nina.

Better still, you might like to try cooking one or more of the following Indian recipes. Boys as well as girls might try this, as Indian boys enjoy helping their mother cook.

Here are two Indian menus the Shah family often cook.

MENU 1: Pulau Rice. Rasgullas. Barfi.

Pulau Rice

Ingredients required:

1½ ozs. ghee (if not, butter).

8–12 ozs., of long grain rice, cooked.

1 tablespoon of chopped toasted almonds.

1 onion and parsley.

½ lb. cooked peas, salt, lemon juice or lemon.

Heat the ghee gently in a frying pan, add the chopped onion and stir until transparent. Add the cooked rice and peas as well as the salt and lemon. Sprinkle with almonds and parsley. Serve and eat.

Rasgulla

Ingredients required:

Plain flour.

Milk powder.

Ghee.

Sugar.

Mix the plain flour and milk powder together to form a thick liquid. Melt some ghee in a pan and mix with the thick liquid. Squeeze the thick liquid into round balls, the size a little less than a golf-ball and fry in another pan in ghee. The gas or electricity should be low and as the balls are fried they change from a milky white to a brownish colour. In another saucepan mix a pound of sugar and twice the amount of water. Stir for ten minutes and then place the "balls" on the table and dip them into a bowl of sugared water. Rasgulla is very tasty and is eaten with the main part of the meal, sometimes as a luxury dish.

Barfi

Ingredients required:

1 box of Ostermilk baby powder No. 2.

1 small tin of evaporated milk.

$\frac{1}{2}$ lb. sugar.

$\frac{1}{2}$ pint water.

1 tea-spoon of rose water (bought from the chemist).

4 ozs. of grated almonds.

Mix the tin of milk with the Ostermilk powder in a large saucepan, then mix the water and sugar in another saucepan and bring to the boil. Add the rose water and the rest of the Ostermilk and mix well. Put the whole mixture in any square or round dishes and sprinkle with almonds. The mixture should be placed in the dish in a thin layer. After ten minutes cut the mixture into small two inch cubes and you will find the sweet dish tasty and delicious.

If you really want to cook a splendid Indian dish, and surprise your friends, then try:

MENU 2: Curried Chicken. Chapattis with butter.

Curry

When Indians and Pakistanis make curry, they do not have any particular measures to follow, only the experience that the mother passes on to her daughter: they measure by estimating the amount of ingredients needed for the number of people who are going to share in the meal. Their estimates are rarely wrong and the result is very tasty, although rather hot for many British people.

Ingredients required:
Powdered Termeric.
Powdered Red Chillies.
Salt (Cooking).
Pieces of Onions (From 2 or 3 onions).
Ghee.
Zira (Ground Cummin Seed).

Place the powdered termeric, powdered red chillies, cooking salt and the pieces of onion in a stone pot and crush them together with a thick wooden stick. Now put a few spoonfuls of ghee in a big saucepan (or patila) and when the ghee has melted place the termeric, red chillies, salt and onions in the ghee. Place the saucepan on a low gas and stir the mixture with a large spoon. Continue stirring from the bottom of the saucepan and when the mixture is sufficiently fried put pieces of meat (e.g. chicken) in the saucepan. Continue stirring and mixing all the ingredients together, taking care that the mixture does not stick to the bottom of the saucepan. Remember to stir from the bottom of the mixture. When you find the pieces of meat shrunk, put two or three glasses of water in the saucepan and cover with the lid. The heat should be low throughout the cooking. After half to three-quarters of an hour, when you see that the meat is not raw but cooked properly, turn off the heat and spread some Zira on the curry and after a few minutes the curry will be ready for serving. If during the cooking the water has evaporated and the meat is uncooked, add more water and cover the saucepan with the lid as before.

Chapattis

Some Hindus like them large, some small. Wheatflour is put into a pot or saucepan and a little water is added; the flour is then rubbed with the hands, water is added again and this method is repeated until the flour is thick. When the flour is thick, a small amount is taken and shaped into a small ball. This ball is then pressed in the hand from top and bottom until the shape is round but flat. A **chakla** or wooden round-shaped disc of an inch thickness is then used. The flat piece of flour is placed on the chakla and pressed equally but gently with a wooden roller or **beilon**, the ends of which are held in the hands. The beilon is moved backwards and forwards again and again until the unbaked chapatti is the right thickness. The unbaked chapatti is now placed on a steel disc or **tava** which is placed over the gas ring or fire, and the chapatti is now baked carefully by turning it over from side to side. Some melted ghee is then placed on the chapatti with a spoon.

The chapatti is now ready for eating. Dripping can be used as a substitute for ghee which can be made by simmering butter in a saucepan for 1½–2 hours. It should then be strained through fine muslin and stored in a jar.

The Hindu custom is to eat their food with their fingers and so finger-bowls are provided for use before and during the meal and a bowl of water and a towel are placed nearby for washing the hands after the meal.

A Hindu mother seasons her curry with a mixture of spices and herbs, for example, cummin, termeric. British people who wish to cook a curry dish can buy a curry powder, but for best results it should be one mixed in India such as the Madras Curry powder.

Before you begin inviting your British and Indian friends to an Indian meal, be wise and try the recipes out at home with the help of your mother. You will then know what you have to do for a larger group of people rather than the four or five in your own family. You will also know better the quantities that are required for your friends' and your own taste.

If you know of any Indian person who is able to give you advice, ask for his or her help and you will all enjoy the meal much better.

When you have cooked your first Indian meal, then ask your parents to invite your friends round to your house. Perhaps one of your Hindu friends might do the same for you at a later date.

First you will need to think out the menu. Plan this carefully and write it down on a piece of paper.

If you have time, you need to find out all you can about the part of India where your

Hindu friends lived before they came to Britain, so that you can ask them sensible questions about their homeland and then you can learn more interesting things from them. When your Hindu friends invite you to a meal they can ask you questions about places in Britain and so they can learn from you.

You can also decorate the room where you have the meal with pictures, reconstructions of Indian life and flags of India. You can use the colours of the Indian flag to decorate the room as well as having flowers and other decorations you can make yourself.

The British girls who serve the meal can wear saris and you can all sit on the floor to eat the meal.

After the meal, you can arrange for a Hindu father or teacher in the district near your home or school to talk to you about his country and its customs and to allow you to ask questions about India.

The Hindu children can act out little plays about Indian life and the British can share some of the parts. Indian legends and tales can be told simply and then acted, and Indian songs can be learnt and sung.

14   **LALITA'S DRESS**

The **sari**, worn by Lalita and Indian women most of the time, in Britain as in India, is made of silk or nylon, cotton or artificial silk. Its length is six yards. The material has a variety of colours and can be bought in Britain, special shops being opened by the Indians in the large towns and a wide choice of material can be obtained.

In wearing a sari the Indian woman first puts on an Indian type skirt matching the colour of the sari to be worn. This skirt is put on from the waist to a little above the ankles.

A sari has a print design or a design embroidered on the border. The whole of the inside border below has a long piece of material sewn on to it to make the flowing border heavier around the legs. This prevents the lower part of the sari from flying up when the wind is strong.

One end of the sari is now tied by means of a simple knot to the other side of the sari near the navel. This is done by taking the material round the waist from behind the right to the left side. The upper ends of the sari round the waist are carefully tucked in the skirt to allow the flowing border of the sari to cover the ankles and to allow the material to be at the same level all the way round. Great care should be taken over this.

The four yards of the sari to the right of the navel are pleated by the right hand fingers and tucked in the skirt near the navel. The flowing border is automatically pleated.

Now the remaining part of the sari to the right of the pleated and tucked material should be thrown behind the left shoulder covering the front of the body from below the legs to the left shoulder.

SARI

DOPATTA

It is very interesting to watch an Indian woman putting on her sari, so if you know an Indian family very well ask the mother to show you how she does it.

Another form of dress the Indian woman wears is called the **shalwar** or **salwar**. These are trousers gathered in at the ankles worn with a tunic frock, or jumper, or shirt. There is also a separate garment called a **dopatta** to cover the head.

Bracelets, bangles and other jewellery are part of the marriage dowry and are the sole property of the married woman.

Jewellery is given by the parents of the bride at the time of her marriage. The husband also buys her gifts at this time and afterwards whenever he can afford it, as he wants to please his wife.

In India goldsmiths have a regular trade to prepare the jewellery when it is ordered. Some shops sell manufactured jewellery, others sell hand-made. There are some Indians in Britain who know the art of making jewellery and have orders given to them by other Indians living here.

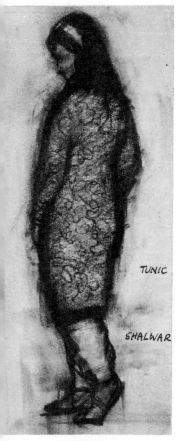

TUNIC

SHALWAR

LALITA'S DRESS

15

A WEDDING

One evening Nina and Nimish were sitting with their mother round a fire. No one had spoken for a few minutes and Lalita was about to leave the room when Nina said, "Mummy, tell us about your wedding in India."

"Oh, Nina, that will take a long time. I suppose you want to stay up later to-night. However, if you both want to listen, I'll tell you."

"Yes, please," said the children.

"When I was eighteen years old," said their mother, "and I had left school, my parents began to think about the man I should marry.

"When I was nearly twenty, they found him. They asked me whether I would marry him, and I was given the chance to say 'no'. We were also allowed to see each other. My parents then announced our engagement and invitation cards were sent out to friends and relatives. Uncles and aunts helped to pay for the festivities. It was a very happy and important occasion in our lives.

"I was very excited, for I wanted to get married and wear my wedding sari and have a red spot on the centre of my forehead. As you know, this spot is mainly used on social occasions and is made with red powder which can be washed off.

"My wedding sari was made of coloured silk woven with real gold thread. This should remind you that before the 17th century India was one of the richest countries in the world, and Indian spices, muslin, silk, pearls and gems were sought after in the markets of Europe. I am very proud of my wedding sari because it is so lovely.

"My father and mother gave me a dowry of money, jewellery, clothes and a great deal of kitchen equipment. Daddy gave me some gifts including some jewellery.

"We waited four months before our wedding day, and during that time we prepared everything for our home. Some of our friends waited only two to three months, but we did not mind waiting a little longer as we were so busy. The marriage ceremony was going to be at my house.

"The wedding day arrived and many of our relatives and friends came to wish us happiness. My father was the oldest man on my side of the family so he had to say these words: 'We have gathered here to betroth Lalita and Narinder to form ties of love and companionship and to respect each other, so that they may grow spiritually'.

"The ceremony took a very long time, because at every step prayers were offered to God in the presence of the Sacred Fire as a witness of our vows to live together for our own material and spiritual welfare, for that of our family and for the entire universe."

Nina interrupted: "What actually happened, then, Mummy?"

"There were three stages in this ceremony: the first consisted of prayers to God and the deities or other gods; the second stage was our reception where the blessings and good wishes of the elders were given; and the third stage again consisted of prayer to God and the deities.

"In the second stage, my parents solemnly offered me as a gift to my husband by placing my hand on his, which showed our love for each other.

"My brother also poured fried rice on my

hands to show that he gave his consent and approval to our marriage.

"My husband and I then took seven steps together while we went round the sacrificial fire, and these steps reminded us that we were to remain faithful to each other in heart, mind and soul, and that we would never break these vows.

"At the seventh step the ceremony was almost completed and we said to each other:

'Into my will I take thy heart,
Thy mind shall follow mine,
Let the heart of yours be mine
And the heart of mine be yours.'

"Finally we looked up to the Pole-star with a prayer which showed our longing for continued companionship between us throughout our life.

"This was followed by prayer to God and the deities, and blessings were asked of God on the elders, friends, and well-wishers who attended the ceremony and witnessed the marriage. Everyone then expressed their best wishes before we left for our honeymoon.

"When you two children grow up, I hope you will be as happy as your father and I are, even though **you** may have a more simple wedding.'

After reading about Lalita's wedding, find out if your own parents were married in a Church. If so, you will find the service that was used in the Book of Common Prayer. This service has been used for very many years in Britain, but when Narinder and Lalita were married in India everything was very different. Even the way in which Lalita was chosen to be Narinder's wife was an old Indian custom which you may think is unusual

Not all Hindus come over to Britain as a

family, for many male Gujaratis and Punjabis, although married before they arrive here, prefer to come alone at first, to save enough money and then to bring over their wife and children.

Lately, however, younger men have been coming to Britain, and their brides have come over to get married. In a case like this there are two weddings; one in India and one in Britain, where the man and wife are present.

Families in India dislike their sons or daughters marrying Europeans, and therefore, male immigrants arrive here with the idea that they do not mix with white women.

If a Hindu follows his traditional beliefs, he is forbidden to marry anyone except one who is also of this Hindu belief. If he married a white person his marriage would not be considered pure. This belief is not his religious belief. Nowhere in the Hindu Scripture is this belief written, but it has been practised under the influence of the caste system.

Hindu girls of eleven are not expected to mix with any boys, and although most British parents may not mind a British boy going out with an Indian girl, by tradition an Indian girl's parents do not wish her to go out with him.

Many Hindus are beginning to think that a change in this attitude might help British people to understand Hindus better, for where people are able to talk and share experiences, they are better able to work and live in the same community. It is, however, a difficult problem.

In Britain, as in India, a Hindu is not allowed to marry outside his caste, and if the woman were not a Hindu, then the marriage would be looked at in a worse light. The man is not made an outcaste now. He was made an outcaste in the past, and if the family continued to see him, then they too would be outcaste. Even if they have nothing to do with him, they would probably be made to perform social and ritual penances and in addition pay a fine if they wished to remain in the caste. Now this is not so.

But Indian law says that a man does not lose his share in the joint family property even if he is outcaste or changes his religion. An outcaste, however, will not receive any help from the family or society which would enable him to receive his share. At the same time, he may not have the spare money to go to law about his claims.

But often before this situation worsens, the family and close relatives will do their best to prevent such a marriage and in most cases the Hindu man's family ties, from the point of view of money, property and love for his family are strong enough to prevent him from disgracing his family.

If a Hindu does marry a British girl, in Britain, he is not expelled by the immigrant community. The newly married couple still find friends in the community and are welcome in the immigrants' homes. There are many examples of this in Britain.

Their marriage, however, is not accepted as the marriage of two immigrants would be, and sometimes rude remarks from a few orthodox immigrants hurt the couple, though they continue to share the community's life.

They are able to take part in the Hindu community's activities and get normal help when it is needed. It is the British girl or boy who decides whether or not they keep the link with the Hindu community. The Hindu communities under British and Western influence have successfully made new patterns of ways of living, and, therefore, it is easier for them to make British people welcome.

A religious-minded Hindu believes that according to his previous **karma**, or existence, a special person is destined for him or her and that his parents must find that special person.

The parents have to match approximately the age, temperament, education and background of the man and woman whom they want married and often the man waits for years before his partner is found. Even in Britain, Hindu men are waiting for a letter from their parents to say that a woman has been found for them.

If a good match is found by the parents in India, then the couple will marry in India. If the couple are married in Britain, they are not welcomed back in India, as they do not have the same customs and home background as the Indian Hindus.

At one time the man and the woman were not allowed to meet each other until the wedding ceremony, but nowadays they are allowed to meet their future partner. Whatever they may feel, they very rarely, if ever, say that they will not marry the partner chosen for them.

Hindu young people say about this: "After all, our parents have given us birth, nourishment and education; we owe them our very life. They will do whatever is best for us."

B SUGGESTIONS AND QUESTIONS

These are not questions you **have** to answer and the suggestions are not things you **have** to do. Choose something in which you are really interested and do your best to enjoy what you have chosen.

Things to Find Out
Find out about any festivals or special celebrations that are held in your city, town, or village. Talk about one particular festival to someone who knows nothing about it. Let the person who listens to you ask you questions about that festival.

Things to Plan
Plan a class festival based on Indian customs to celebrate the end of term and perform it in front of another class. You might use some of the material suggested in the section on page 79.

Things to Make

a. When you have made an Indian meal and invited your Hindu friends to eat it, help them to plan and prepare a British meal.

b. Listen to some Indian music on a record and then make up your own dance to go with the music.

c. Dress up a doll in Indian National Costume. Have a fashion parade with several dolls, and select the one you think is the best.

d. Collect as many Indian poems as you can, and make your own poetry book. You may like to read these poems to your class.

Books to Read

What other religions, beside the Christian and Hindu religions, are there? Read about them in books and encyclopaedias, which you will find in your class and school libraries. Talk about them with others.

From what you have read so far, make up some more questions of your own, perhaps with the help of your teacher, and try to discover the answers through your parents, your teachers, and your library books.

16 NARINDER

There is a story about the Parsees who lived many years ago in Iran. They were being persecuted in their own land for their religious beliefs, so they decided they would leave Iran and cross over to India and ask if they might live in Gujarat, the land north of Bombay.

The leader of the Parsees sent a message to the local Raja asking his permission to stay in the area where the Raja lived. The Raja sent him back a glass of water filled to the brim. The Parsee added sugar to the water and sent it back.

The Raja was pleased when he tasted the water and found it sweet, because he knew from this action that the Parsees would mix with his people as sugar does with water. They would become one with the people of Gujarat.

The Parsees did in fact become one with the Gujaratis, yet they were able to keep their own religion, their own culture and their own way of living, and were accepted by the Gujaratis as a people in their own right, living peacefully and lawfully amongst another people with a different background and a different way of thinking.

Perhaps when Narinder decided to leave his own country and live in Britain he thought and hoped that he and his family might live in the same way as the Parsees did in Gujarat. He knew that for many decades Indians had migrated to nearly all the lands under British rule and that they had worked as agricultural labourers, craftsmen, unskilled workers and traders.

Most of the Indians then came from certain areas in India, and now in the 20th century those Indians who come to Britain come

from particular regions like the Gujarat and the Punjab.

This does mean, though, that the Indians who come to live in Britain have the same language, the same culture and the same family ties as those who have arrived before them, and they know that they will be welcomed and provided for when they first arrive in a strange land having no home, no work and no friends.

The main reason they are welcomed and cared for when they arrive in this country is because of something called, in India, "the joint family system". This system is not only practised in the villages of India, but also in many other countries of the world.

It means that married brothers and their families and unmarried brothers and sisters live under the protection of the oldest male member of the family, usually the father or grandfather. All belongings are shared between the families, and if the family house is large enough, all the members live in it, but have separate kitchens. Everyone in the family is helped when there is a need, and sacrifices, like doing without when someone else is in greater need, are made willingly.

In Britain this system is still carried out by many Indians, but now, when the grandfather dies, members of the family often split up and have their own homes. This may even be so while the grandfather is still alive and he shares the different homes of the family at different times.

The family in Britain not only remembers and helps those who come into it, but it also remembers those of the family who remain in

India. Money is sent out regularly and it is a matter of pride that it is sent, for not only is the family helped to a better standard of living, but the prestige of the family is raised in the village.

In India, parents and teachers are believed to be next to God in importance. Every day a Hindu boy or man touches the feet of his parents and teachers; the girls only touch their mother's feet. When a boy is old enough to marry, he brings his bride to his father's home and believes that as long as his parents are alive they rule over him: he loves them and receives their blessings.

Old people, in India, do not die of loneliness, because the family is always ready to love and care for them. To call someone old is a compliment and a sign of respect. The family are very close to each other. A son usually hands his earnings to his father and the father looks after the younger man's needs.

Narinder did not mind the kind of work he had, as long as he earned enough money to help his relatives with the mortgage, rates, gas and electricity bills and the food he ate with them. When he was able to earn enough to save, his first thoughts were for a house so that he and his family could live together.

After three years in Britain Narinder saved enough money to put down a deposit on a mortgage for a house. He obtained the remainder of the money from a Building Society.

He lives in a large town among his own people so that they can continue their Indian customs and culture and all meet in a cinema that they have had bought for their own entertainment. Here he is able to buy Indian newspapers and food, and meet and entertain his own friends and other Indians from another district. This, of course, does not prevent him from going to British entertainments and buying British food, but it does help him to miss his own homeland less, and to feel he can talk to people who understand his way of thinking. It also helps him to remember and keep the Indian customs, habits and language. It gives him the opportunity to hear and practise Indian folk music, dance and song; to practise painting, drawing and sculpture; to organise his own way of living, and to take on the responsibility of social work amongst his own people, as well as to invite his British friends to share his entertainment.

Narinder does not want to keep it secret that he is here to earn money and that he is prepared to work hard for it. He is willing to work Saturdays and Sundays and to do over-time, so that, although he earns less money from the basic rate of pay than a British worker in the same job, he really earns more because he does more over-time. He spends less and he drinks less. He tries to keep himself healthy and does not waste what he has.

Narinder believes that it is as important for him to be himself, and not a carbon copy of the British people around him, as it is for him and the British people to talk together and find out for themselves about each other's ways and customs.

How can this be done? Narinder says that this can be done in quite simple ways to begin with; first, a smile as you queue up in the supermarket, or as you wait for a bus, or as you go into the class-room, or as you leave your house in the morning. A smile is the language of friendship in any country in the world, and Indians know what it means even though they may not be able to speak the English language themselves. They may be struggling with a few words that they have picked up from a sympathetic British man, woman or child, or even from their own children who are taught in British schools.

Another simple way is to say "Hullo" or "Good morning", or even, as many British people like to do, to make a remark about the weather. Of course, if you have Indian boys or girls in your class or form, you can do the same as you would for your British friends. Ask them to join in your games or to share your hobbies, or if you get really friendly, to share your secrets. Let them feel that they are part of the school like you, and that they are as welcome as your own British friends.

But what Narinder is saying is not always easy. Not all British people get on with other British people, and it is sometimes even more difficult when you do not always understand the reason why someone says or does something, and more difficult still when a person comes from a different land with different customs and ideas.

The best thing is to try and understand them more. When you are not sure what to do or say, it is important to wait in case you say or do anything that you will feel sorry about later. Try to get to know your Indian friends by inviting them round to your house, and don't forget to let your mother know too, so that she can welcome them as well.

17 INDIAN CHILDREN

The Hindus love children. In India they are often born into a family even though the mother and father know it will be difficult for them to feed and clothe them. The children are brought up to respect not only their parents, but all adults. Age, they are told, is a mark of wisdom, youth a mark of inexperience. If the parents die before the children are old enough to look after themselves the remainder of the adult family care for them as if they were their own children. Hindu children are brought up strictly whoever looks after them, and in normal conditions they lead as happy a life as most other children. Of course things are very different when there is a famine.

One of the most important things that a Hindu child must learn is to read and write. Indian parents and teachers do not mind whether they can speak fluently, but they must be able to read and write, and more attention is paid to reading and writing than to speaking, and that is one reason why Indian children find it difficult to speak English. They are not used to speaking naturally and fluently like English children, and are not trained to speak in drama and other lessons.

Indian children are hard-working, but they find it difficult to understand the accents of British people. In India they may have been taught to write correct English, but they have had few British people to teach them in school from the age of ten or eleven. English in India has depended very much on religious organisations like missionary societies and on private schools. Under these British teachers the English accent of the Indians has been good, but English is poorly spoken by the majority of Indians.

Hindu children under eleven years of age, and particularly those who enter a British school at the age of five years, are able to learn the English language quite easily and are able to act as interpreters for their parents when their parents need to speak to people in positions of authority, like Head Teachers and Local Government Officers.

The parents from the Punjab speak Punjabi and those from Gujarat speak Gujarati, but they are not able to understand each other's language, so they have to speak another language to make themselves understood, and that is either English, of which they speak very little at first, or Hindi-Urdu.

Modern India recognises fourteen major languages, twenty-four minor languages and twenty-three tribal languages, spoken by 100,000 people or more, and seven hundred and twenty languages or dialects spoken by less than 100,000 people.

The boundaries of the modern States of India are drawn according to the main languages spoken in the area, so that Bengali is the language of West Bengal, Punjabi that of the Punjab, Hindi that of Uttar Pradesh, and Gujarati that of the Gujarat area.

Urdu, Hindustani and Hindi are spoken by about one hundred and fifty million people, but the official languages of modern India which are used in all official documents and speeches are Hindi and English. Hindi has been influenced in the past by Sanskrit and Persian; Urdu, which is the official language of Pakistan, is a mixture of Hindi, Persian and Arabic.

Education is felt by the parents to be very important. In India, both rich and poor people want their children to be educated properly and until the children are about thirteen years old the parents have to pay for this education, and so it is impressed upon the children that they must not waste their time at school, but must work hard and do their very best. Every parent wants his son to be in a white-collar job where he can have a pension and know that he has a job for the rest of his life if he works hard.

If Nina and Nimish had been at school in India they would have learnt Hindi, which instead of twenty-six letters has sixty-one letters in its alphabet. But some British boys and girls may think that the Hindi language is easier to learn than English, especially when it has to be written, as Hindi is a phonetic system of writing, and the words are written exactly as they sound.

In English we learn that "tough" is spelled "t-o-u-g-h" although it sounds as though it should be spelled "t-u-f".

How much easier English spelling would be if it were spelt exactly as it sounded, and how much more difficult it is for Hindu children to learn how to spell English words.

Nina and Nimish write their letters from left to right as their British friends do, but in Hindi after the letters of a word are put together, they must have a straight line over them, touching the heads of the letters in the word. This shows that the word has been completed.

Here are some of the letters of the Hindi alphabet:

A अ, म्र B ब्य C स, क

D	ड	E	इ	F	फ
G	ग, ज	H	ह	I	इ
J	ज	K	क	L	ल
M	म	N	न	O	ओ
P	प	Q	क	R	र
S	स	T	ट	U	उ
V	व	W	व	X	क्स
Y	ई	Z	ज़		

Here are a few simple words in Hindi:

boy: लड़का   girl: लड़की

school: स्कूल   teacher: अद्यायक

lessons: पाठ   books: पुस्तकें, किताबें

paper: काग़ज़   pen: कलम

pencil: पेंसिल, पेनसिल   ruler: फुटरूल, फुटरूल

the: वो   a: एक

there is: वहां है   there are: वहां हैं

The Hindi word for "the" is the nearest possible meaning.

18

NINA AND NIMISH

In Britain, Hindu children are given the same education as British children are, and this is free.

Nina is in a Primary School. She is in one of the Upper Junior classes and is able to speak English as well as the British children in her class. She has been in the Primary School since her fifth birthday and has joined in all the English games and lessons that the British children have experienced.

When she first arrived at the Infants School with her mother she felt very strange and did not go near anybody. She stayed in a part of the classroom where no other children were sitting or standing, and cried. Her teacher was very kind, but she did not make her join in what the other children were doing. She just allowed her to watch until Nina was ready to play with the other boys and girls. For two or three days she watched and then she became interested in two boys playing with some very large bricks. She watched from a distance at first, then gradually she went nearer, and at last touched one of the bricks. The two boys were pleased to see her come to them and they let her build a house with them.

Gradually Nina became more interested in what the other children were doing, especially when they were acting nursery rhymes and stories and speaking in a strange language. Later she joined in the fun, and as the term came to an end she had made some friends.

As Nina grew older she asked her friends to come to her home, and there they played games, and laughed and teased each other as all good friends do. Her British friends then asked her to their home, and their parents made her welcome. Sometimes her father Narinder took her friends and herself out in the car for a ride and they enjoyed running in the park or walking round the shops.

To Nina life was good, although, of course, it had its difficult times when she was not able to do her work as well as she wanted and when she did not understand some of the things that were said and could not play games as well as some of the other girls. But she began to realise gradually that she was just like anyone else in the class.

Her brother Nimish was not so fortunate. He is in a Secondary School now, but he felt as Nina felt when he was in the Primary School. Somehow it is different now. It is not that the teachers are any less kind in the Secondary School than they were in the Primary. It is not that the work is any less interesting, he enjoys it very much, but some of the boys in his school do not appear to want to talk to him, and as he leaves school at the end of the day he walks alone, so different from the days of his Primary School when they all walked out together and enjoyed each other's company.

After he started at the Secondary School he began to wonder why there was this feeling of unfriendliness and why no one asked him out to their homes after school. He knew that many of the boys belonged to clubs, societies and churches and that the boys in his class played football matches in their clubs against other organisations. Why, he thought to himself, did not the churches ask him to join in their social activities, or the Scouts in theirs? Why did people want to be separate and not mix together?

Nimish wanted to be part of the society in which he lived. He was proud of the achievements of his school and proud of the part he played in it, and he appreciated the efforts of his teachers to encourage the mixing of all boys in the playground, and of the Head Teacher in bringing together all the parents and helping them to mix freely and speak to each other.

Nimish did not want any special favours. He just wanted the opportunity to take part in any activity in which he was interested and to which he was able to contribute. If he was good at playing a musical instrument, then he wanted to be in the orchestra playing on special occasions, but if there was someone better than himself then he would not mind, for that was only fair to the other boy. He felt the same about the football and hockey teams. What he did not want was a competition between the British and the Indians in the class, nor did he want separate classes for immigrants unless they were for a short time to enable the immigrants to learn the English language more quickly. What he did want was to be treated just as any other boy, and he hoped that when he left School he would be given an equal opportunity to get a job in the same way as his class-mates.

He is going to do his best at school now, so that his hopes will come true.

19

AN INDIAN FABLE

The British read stories like Grimm's Fairy Tales; the Hindus read stories from the **Panchatantra**. These stories have been translated into many languages and the story that follows is in Hindi with an English translation and is told by Mr. S. N. Bharadwaj, President of the Hindu Centre, London, who is a qualified teacher in a Secondary School in Southall, Middlesex.

The Lion and The Hare

There lived a lion in a forest. He was very cruel. He killed more animals than he could eat. One day all the animals met together. They said, "The lion kills so many of us every day. After some time there will be no animal left in the forest. This will be bad for the lion as well. Why should we not ask the lion to kill only one of us every day?"

All the animals agreed and the fox was sent to the lion. The fox told the lion their decision. The lion agreed.

From that day on, the lion would get an animal every day. He was very happy, and so were the animals. One day it was the turn of the hare to go. The hare did not reach the lion's den in time. The lion was very hungry. He felt very angry. He thought the animals had not kept their word. Then late in the afternoon, he saw a small hare coming very slowly. The lion shouted at the hare and said, "Why are you so late?"

The hare looked frightened and said, "It is not my fault, Sir. I met another lion on the way. He wanted to eat me. I said, 'You shouldn't eat me, because I am food for the King of the Forest.' "

सिंह और खरगोश

किसी वन में एक सिंह रहता था। वह
बड़ा निर्दयी था। उसके भोजन के लिये एक ही
पशु काफ़ी था, किन्तु वह व्यर्थ ही बहुत से
पशु मार दिया करता था। एक दिन सभी पशु
मिल कर कहने लगे- यह सिंह हर रोज़ इतने
पशु मार देता है। कुछ समय के बाद हम में से
एक भी न बचेगा। यह बात तो सिंह के लिये
भी बुरी होगी। हमें सिंह को कहना चाहिये कि
वह हम में से एक को हर रोज़ खा लिया करे।

सभी यह बात मान गये। एक लूमड़ी को
सिंह के पास भेजा गया। लूमड़ी से पशुओं का
निर्णय सुन कर सिंह मान गया।

सिंह के पास हर रोज़ एक पशु पहुंच
जाता। सिंह और पशु प्रसन्न रहने लगे। एक
दिन खरगोश की बारी आ गयी। वह ठीक
समय पर सिंह की गुफा में न पहुंचा। सिंह को
भूख सता रही थी। उसे क्रोध आ रहा था। वह
सोचने लगा कि पशुओं ने अपने वचन का
पालन नहीं किया। खरगोश धीरे धीरे आता
दिखायी दिया। तब तो दोपहर हो चुकी थी।

सिंह ने चिल्ला कर कहा- तूने इतनी देर
क्यों की? भय से कांपते हुए खरगोश बोला-
जनाब, मेरा कोई दोष नहीं। आपके पास आते
हुए राह में कोई दूसरा सिंह मिल गया था।
वह मुझे खाना चाहता था। मैंने कहा- मुझे
न खाइए, मैं तो वन के राजा का भोजन हूं।

When the lion heard that there was another lion in the forest, he was more angry than before. He said, "Is there another lion in this forest?"

The hare said, "Yes Sir, there is. He calls himself the King of the Forest. The King of the Forest said, 'Bring your King to me and I shall teach him a lesson.' And so, Sir, I have come to you."

"Oh!" said the foolish lion, "I must kill that beast first. Take me to him."

The clever hare took the lion to an old well and said, "That lion lives down here. You can call him up, if you please."

The lion looked into the well and saw his own face in the water. He roared and heard a loud roar in return. He thought that the lion in the well was challenging him. It made him so angry that he roared louder and jumped into the well.

The hare looked down into the well, laughed loudly and ran back to the other animals to give them the good news.

AN INDIAN FABLE

सिंह ने उसी वन में किसी और सिंह के
बारे जब यह बात सुनी तो उसका क्रोध
और बढ़ गया। उसने पूछा- इस वन में दूसरा
क्या कोई सिंह भी है ?

खरगोश बोला, जी हां, रहता है। वह
भी अपने आप को वन का राजा कहता है।
उस वन के राजा ने मुझे कहा- अपने राजा
को मेरे पास ले कर आ, मैं उसका दिमाग
ठीक कर दूंगा। सो मैं आप के पास आया हूं।

मूर्ख सिंह बोला- तो यह बात है। मैं
पहले उसी को ही मारूंगा। मुझे उसके ले चल पास।

चालाक खरगोश सिंह को एक पुराने
कुंए के पास ले गया। कहा- महाराज, वह
सिंह उसी जगह नीचे रहता है। आप चाहें
तो आवाज़ दे कर उसे ऊपर बुला सकते हैं।

सिंह ने कुंए के अन्दर झांका। उसे अपना
मुख जल में दिखाई दिया। वह गरजने
लगा, उसे भी गूंज सुनाई दी। उसने
सोचा कुंए वाला सिंह उसे ललकार रहा है।
उसे इतना क्रोध आया कि ऊंचे ऊंचे
गरजते हुए कुंए में कूद गया। खरगोश, कुंए में
झांका, खूब हंसा और पशुओं को शुभ
समाचार सुनाने दौड़ता हुआ वापिस चला गया।

C SUGGESTIONS AND QUESTIONS

These are not questions you **have** to answer and the suggestions are not things you **have** to do. Choose something in which you are really interested and do your best to enjoy what you have chosen.

Things to Find Out

a. Do the local Scouts, Guides, Churches, or Youth Clubs help to welcome Hindus or any other immigrants? If not, what can you do about it?

b. How do British families care for individual members of the family? In particular, what can be done to help older people who cannot help themselves, or handicapped children, whose parents need time to shop or to do work in the house? Is it possible to form a group of willing people who will help the elderly and the handicapped? Will you help?

Things to Plan

Plan to meet together with some Hindus or other immigrants, get to know them, arrange to take them to your home, and if you go out in the car at the week-end take one of your immigrant friends with you.

Things to Make

Speech helps us to tell other people what
we are thinking and what we want. If we are
on holiday in a foreign country, what
difficulties do we have if we do not speak the
language? How do we overcome the
difficulties and how can we be helped?
Make a book called: "Tips for people visiting
a foreign country." Illustrate this, and then
discuss how you can help someone who
speaks no English or very little, and who
lives in Britain.

Books to Read

Read some stories from India: e.g. "Indian
Tales" by Elizabeth Sharpe; "Indian Fairy
Tales" by Mulk Raj Anand. Compare these
stories with British fables and legends which
you will find in your library.

From what you have read so far, make up
some more questions of your own, perhaps
with the help of your teacher and try to
discover the answers through your parents,
your teachers, and your library books.

20 CUSTOMS AND BEHAVIOUR

Narinder and Lalita have been brought up in India on customs and ways of behaviour that have been taught for very many years. Quite naturally they do not want, nor are they able, to give up all that their parents and teachers have taught them. So it is not surprising that, although Hindus in Britain have adopted some British customs and forms of behaviour, they have not given up all that they practised before they left India. Their children will be in a different position, particularly if they have started schooling in British Primary Schools: they will have been taught British ways by British teachers and children as well as Indian customs and behaviour by their parents.

The British have a saying: "Cleanliness is next to godliness." Hindus would agree that this is a very good rule of conduct, for they lay a great emphasis on the cleanliness of a person's body.

In Britain today there are still many homes where there is no bath, and the toilets are outside the house. Sixty or seventy years ago in Europe a bath was considered a luxury. In India today there is a bathing place in every home, but there are many homes where there are no modern baths as we have in Britain. To a Hindu, taking a bath every day has always been a habit, and very important to him.

His custom has been not to have breakfast without saying his prayers, and his religion tells him not to say his prayers until he has first bathed. He prefers flowing water to still water in a bath, and in some of the big Indian cities there is a rush down to the nearest river between five and six o'clock in the morning to bathe and then to worship in the temples along the river banks before having breakfast and going to work.

In Britain, Indians have baths as we do in our own houses, but they prefer showers which are popular in America and used by people in Britain and Europe on camping sites and in some homes. Showers are preferred because Hindus do not like to wash themselves in water which has become dirty while they are bathing themselves.

Indians have a certain way of thinking about the human body. For instance, because the feet are the lowest part of the body, touching the feet of someone is a way of showing respect for that person.

Because the head is the highest part of the body, what covers the head has special meaning to the Hindu. This is why displacing or hitting a Hindu's headgear amounts to insulting him.

Since food in India is generally eaten with the hands, particular care is taken to keep them clean and to ensure that only the right hand is used for eating as the left hand is considered to be comparatively unclean. In Britain, Hindus sometimes eat with their hands and at other times eat with knives and forks as we do.

They greet each other with the word "Namaste" or "Namaskar" and fold their hands together in greeting. "Namaste" means "I bow before you". These greetings are used at all times of the day and in all situations, but when they meet someone who is not a Hindu they smile, shake hands and bow slightly, addressing them in very polite terms.

Hindus wear similar clothes to British men in India, especially if they know that they

are leaving the homeland for Britain. When they live in Britain they do not wear Indian clothing.

The women, however, keep their Indian dress and most of them wear a sari, but some women from the Punjab wear silk pyjamas, a long shirt and a veil. Very few women adopt British clothing except when they want to find a job; on social occasions they wear their Indian clothing.

Hindu women also use a few cosmetics and scents which are different from those used by British women.

In Britain, as in India, Hindus are required, if they are faithful to their own beliefs, to remember and practise five daily duties in their homes. They are:

1. To worship God by thinking quietly about him and by practising yoga which is the highest form of worship.
2. To worship God by ritual or ceremony by honouring the powers of God in nature.
3. To pay respect and make offerings to their elders who are living now while at the same time remembering their ancestors.
4. To offer hospitality to unexpected guests and gifts to those in need.
5. To feed all creatures, such as birds, cats and dogs (in India cows and ants would be included).

In India, Hindus take off their shoes before they enter a place of worship, because they do not want to take the dirt and germs on their shoes into the Temple. In Britain, their place of worship is usually a hall hired from a local church or organisation where they do not take off their shoes.

According to the Hindu Scriptures, sixteen purifying rites or "samskaras" should be given to every Hindu at various stages of his life. In Britain, only four are performed by the guru or priest.

First a few weeks after the child's birth, the naming ceremony is performed. The child is given a name according to the dominant planet at the time of his birth, and is then taken out of the house into the sunlight for the first time. After a while, depending on its health, solid food is given by the mother to the child for the first time.

Secondly, the first hair of the child is clipped to symbolise the removal of any spiritual evil or physical uncleanness that the child may have brought from a previous life.

The third and fourth rites are the marriage ceremony and cremation at death.

COMMUNITY LIFE

Not all Indians who come to Britain can be called immigrants.

Some are visitors who come here on holiday or on business; others are students who go to College or University; still others are qualified doctors who come to Britain for further study in our hospitals, or who are officials of the High Commission of India. These people are not likely to become permanent citizens of Britain, although they would probably stay for a number of years before returning to India.

Those who are said to be immigrants are those Indians who come to Britain to work in order to pay for their stay and to earn money. They are unskilled or semi-skilled workers. Although they do not always intend to stay in this country for the rest of their lives, they often change their minds and decide to become permanent residents of Britain.

It is they who form themselves into communities or groups of people who share ideas and experiences. These communities are closed to other people, even to Indians who do not come from the same regions in India and who do not have similar standards of behaviour.

Indians coming to Britain make for their own village-kin group, which means that where they decide to live and work there are other immigrants from their own village or region who are of the same caste and who are relatives.

When the Shah family arrived here, they found accommodation with a relative (or he could have been a fellow-villager), and quite naturally they found themselves doing the

same things and joining in the same activities as the others in the group, as well as speaking the same language as those around them.

It does happen sometimes that an Indian who speaks English or Hindi-Urdu makes friends with someone who does not speak his own regional language but who does speak one of the other two languages. But the village-kin or caste friendships are stronger because they are not confined to one British town but may be scattered all over the country.

When Narinder and Lalita are on holiday they keep in touch with any relatives or friends by visiting them in their own homes. The Shahs are always welcomed wherever they go and are often able to make new friends outside their village-kin group but within their community.

These friends, too, help a Hindu when he is looking for a job, for they will provide him with food and accommodation and in many cases will help him get the work he wants.

When large groups of immigrants live and work in an area of a town or city, they form a kind of club or association. In Britain, these associations are of two kinds. One kind is formed to help keep the immigrants together, because when they were in India they lived outside the towns and in the country, and felt a closeness for one another which is seldom found among people who live in towns.

Hindus like to be together to talk to each other and be entertained. It enables them to keep loyal to each other and to help each other, even though this may lead to overcrowding in their homes.

COMMUNITY LIFE   103

Hindus, with other Indians, are willing to form an Indian Workers Association to collect money and hire or buy a building such as a cinema that is no longer wanted by the British community. This is what Narinder and his friends have done.

The other kind of association is mainly political and helps leaders from the Indian community to get in touch with the British Authorities over the many problems that arise out of a shortage of houses or out of race prejudice, education, employment and medical treatment.

The association tries its best to see that its members are treated justly and do not lose the rights, privileges and responsibilities that are theirs as members living in a free and democratic country.

All Indians are trying to adjust themselves to a fast, indoor urban life when they have been used to a slow, out-of-door rural life. There is a great awareness of the image of their community and they do not want this image spoiled, so they avoid going to the police when they quarrel among themselves and instead ask the older members of the community or a professional Indian, such as a doctor or lawyer, to settle their differences.

Narinder finds that although some British people are friendly, others are unfriendly at work, unfriendly at helping him to find lodgings, and that they do not encourage any of his efforts to join in their recreations or amusements.

Neither he nor Lalita knows the British way of life well, and Narinder has only changed his dress and his eating and spending habits a little, while Lalita rarely appears in anything but a sari and knows very little abou. the English language.

But Nina and Narinder, their children, who are in British schools now, will know the British way of life better; they will be able to speak English more fluently and they will have shared in the many activities of British boys and girls at school.

They hope that they will have had a chance to visit British homes and invite British boys and girls into their homes and share common interests before they become adults. They also hope that "the sugar will be put into the water", and that the two communities, British and Hindu, will learn to grow closer together and form an open society where they can meet and enjoy each other's company.

To achieve this much depends on you, and what you have learnt about their way of life.

D SUGGESTIONS AND QUESTIONS

These are not questions you **have** to answer and the suggestions are not things you **have** to do. Choose something in which you are really interested and do your best to enjoy what you have chosen.

Things to Find Out
a. What Hindu ways of living are like British ways of living?
b. What Hindu ideas are like the Christian way of thinking?
c. What does the author mean when he writes: "It is also to be hoped that 'the sugar will be put into the water?' " (See page 80).

Things to Plan
Why do immigrants come to Britain? How can we help them to feel happier in the town or city where they live? Can we help now? Make a list of ways in which you can do this.

Things to Make
List different British customs and then make a block graph to show how many in your class practise these customs. Compare your graph with that of another class.

Books to Read

Peoples of the world have different beliefs and customs. Discover these from any library books that tell you about them and make your own class book with descriptions, drawings, and pictures. Talk about these beliefs and customs, and compare them with those of the British and Hindu.

From what you have read in this book, make up some more questions of your own, perhaps with the help of your teacher, and try to discover the answers through your parents, your teachers, and your library books. When you have finished this book, you might like to read other books about India or you might like to have displays in your classroom of your models and books about India.

Get together in small groups of three or four and plan what you can do next to help immigrant peoples in Britain.